Learn to read Hebrew in 6 weeks!

LEARN TO READ
HEBREW
IN 6 WEEKS!

WRITTEN BY MIIKO SHAFFIER

SHEFER

PUBLISHING

Written by: Miiko Shaffier
Edited by: Zehava Arky
Illustrated and Designed by: Ken Parker (visual-variables.com)

Published by:
Shefer Publishing
www.SheferPublishing.com

For permissions, comments and ordering information write:
Miiko@LearnHebrew.tv

ISBN 978-0-997-86750-3

THANKS

A most special thanks to my incredible, beloved husband Aaron Shaffier. He encouraged me to try something new and believed I would be adding something valuable to the world.

My gratitude goes to all the wonderful students who attended my live-broadcast classes on Periscope. My students' success and positivity are what led me to write this book.

My confident, cheerful and awesome editor Zehava Arky is greatly appreciated.

Many thanks to Ken Parker for illustrating and designing this book. He was so optimistic and creative! I handed him some rough sketches and a manuscript and he handed me back a beautifully illustrated and designed book which is truly a work of art!

DEDICATED

To the Rebbe and his Shluchim around the world.
—Shirli Reed/Batya Sasson

To the young and old people of all faiths who will benefit from this book.
—Mark and Diane Cowhy

WELCOME

My name is Miiko. I grew up in the USA and Canada but in 2007 I moved to Israel. I'm a mom of nine. One day I heard about a new app called Periscope that lets people broadcast live from their smartphone. Anyone in the world who has that app can tune in and interact with the broadcaster and the other viewers. I immediately thought of how awesome it would be to see other people's worlds broadcasted in real time, and to share my own. I wanted to add something that might be fun AND valuable to people.

A great Rabbi named Menachem Mendel Schneerson once said that everyone should be involved in spreading knowledge. Even if all someone knows is one letter of the alphabet they should teach that letter to someone who doesn't know it. If they know more...well they should teach more! In that way we will ALL enrich the lives of others. So I took his advice literally and I decided to teach the Hebrew alphabet. Hebrew reading actually.

The idea was to teach two live classes a week for six weeks. So I got started! I quickly grew an audience of almost three thousand followers! In just a few short months, hundreds of people had learned to read Hebrew with my live broadcast classes and hundreds more through recorded classes on YouTube. I also made a website called LearnHebrew.tv as a resource for people who'd missed a class or wanted to rewatch something.

From the beginning I heard the same thing from many of my students, "You should make this into a book!" So here it is! In this book, I take the same proven approach I've taken in my online classes to teach you to read Hebrew in just 6 weeks.

It's easy, fast, and fun. I'm always amazed how teachers and authors manage to overcomplicate Hebrew reading. Hebrew is a language with incredible depth and significance, but it's very simple to read! Like any journey that seems insurmountable, the first step is the one to focus on. Once you succeed with the first step, you realize that you CAN take the second step, and you do! It's been incredible to be a part of this exciting process for so many wonderful people. Now it's **YOUR TURN!**

PEP TALK

For so many people, learning Hebrew seems like an unattainable life goal. But I'm here to tell you that it's easy. In this book I'll teach you to read Hebrew in 15-20 minutes, twice a week in just **SIX SHORT WEEKS!**

Reading in Hebrew is the biggest hurdle to learning the Hebrew language. There are so many of my students who say the same thing, "The Hebrew letters were Chinese to me before I started! I can't believe I can read Hebrew now!" But you know what? It was easy for them and you can do it too!

People of all ages and backgrounds have been learning to read Hebrew in six weeks with my system. People with all different kinds of motivations. My favorite part of teaching Hebrew is hearing people's motivations. Whether it's to know the language of the Bible, to communicate with Hebrew speaking grandkids or to prepare for a trip to the Holy Land.

The motivations aren't the only thing that inspires me. I'm honored again and again to hear the success my students find in my method of teaching Hebrew reading. I've had many students who tried other methods and had given up. But somehow, circumstances led them to me and now they are reading Hebrew.

Just take a second and look at your calendar. Pick a milestone about six weeks away. It could be a holiday, New Year's or a birthday. Pick a special event and make that the same day as your Hebrew reading goal! You can and will read Hebrew by that date. You can do it faster too, but six weeks is a comfortable pace for most people.

WEEK ONE

WEEK TWO

WEEK THREE

WEEK FOUR

WEEK FIVE

WEEK SIX

WEEK ONE
LESSON ONE

Let's get started! Let's start by talking about a word in English which is an easy word for people to read. I like to use the word "banana."

In English words are written on a straight line from left to right with the vowels and consonants on the same line. Like in the word banana the 'b' is followed by an 'a' then an 'n' then an 'a' etc.

In Hebrew most vowels hang out BELOW the consonants. Like this:

B N N
A A A

Same word. It's just that the vowels are below the consonants instead of following the consonants. Cool right? Let's use a different word example: "love." Now try to read it like this:

L V
O E

Here's one more: "super."

S P R
U E

That's the first trick of reading in Hebrew. The vowels hang out below the consonants.

Just like in English, there are a lot more consonants than vowels. The few vowels that there are (for the most part) hang out below the line, right under the consonant.

Now let's go back to the first word example that we used "banana." In Hebrew, the words are read from right to left. Try reading the word "banana" from right to left:

ANANAB

It's funny to read from right to left, but the human mind is amazing and you can get used to this funny thing really fast. Just like people in different countries manage just fine to drive on opposite sides of the road. There are entire countries full of people who read from right to left. Entire groups of my students have learned to read from right to left too. I'd say this is the hardest part of the entire language. It really is a simple language.

You can do it!

!TI OD NAC UOY

THESE TWO BASIC DIFFERENCES ARE THE BASIS OF READING IN HEBREW.

REMEMBER:

• THE VOWELS HANG OUT BELOW THE CONSONANTS.
• THE WORDS ARE READ FROM RIGHT TO LEFT.

With that in mind, let's now read "banana":

Read it from right to left.

NNB
AAA

Amazing. Right?! It's a whole new world of reading! Seriously! THESE two differences are THE keys to reading in Hebrew. That big language hurdle you thought you might never overcome? That's it. Now all you have to do is learn which unique shapes represent which sounds. It's going to be awesome. Those six weeks are going to pass whether you do this or not. So let's do it! You'll have an awesome life skill that will be more enlightening than you can yet imagine.

WEEK ONE
LESSON TWO

THE LETTER "BET."

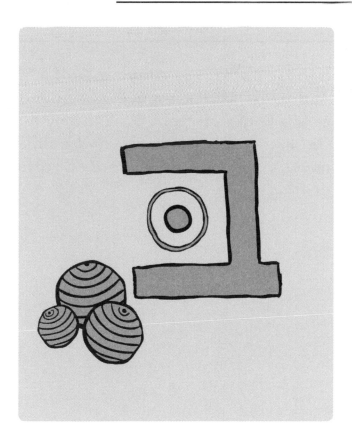

Let's get down to learning some letters! The first letter we're going to learn is the letter "Bet." It looks just like a Ball in a Box. And it makes the sound of the English letter "B." Perfect. Right?

THE LETTER "GIMMEL."

It looks like a **Guy playing Golf**. And guess what? It makes the sound of the English letter "**G**." But only a "**G**" like in the words guy and golf, never a "**G**" like in the words giraffe or fringe.

THE LETTER "DALED."

The letter "Daled" looks like a Door and it makes the sound of the English letter "D."

For now, the names of the letters aren't really important. Concentrate on remembering the sounds the letters make based on how each letter looks.

Today we're also going to learn two vowels. They both make the same sound. That's easy, right!? The first vowel is called "PATACH" and makes the sound of the English letter combination "ah", like the sound you make when you get into a hot jacuzzi. More precisely, it makes the sound of the English letter 'A' in the word far.

The PATACH looks like this:

The second vowel for today Is called a "KAMATZ" and ALSO makes the sound of the English letter combination "ah" or the 'A' in far. How convenient!

The KAMATZ looks like this:

Remember the first rule of Hebrew reading that we learned? "PATACH" and "KAMATZ" ALWAYS hang out BELOW the consonant. And unlike English vowels, Hebrew vowels always make the same sound. It doesn't matter which consonant the vowel follows or proceeds. There are no tricks in Hebrew, and no complicated vowel combinations like in English either.

Think about it, English is a really tricky language! Hebrew is straightforward. There are certainly no words in Hebrew with tricky spelling like 'though', 'thought', 'trough' and 'tough'. Hebrew is a perfectly phonetic language, you read the letters exactly as you see them. That's it.

We can already read some words with the letters we know! Let's give it a try.

בַּד

Let's work through it together. Nice and slow. Start on the right with the ball in the box "**B**." Add to it the vowel hanging out below it "**ah**." Now come back up to the next consonant that looks like a doorway "**D**." We can read the Hebrew word "**BahD**." "**BahD**" means **FABRIC**. You did it!

Reading in Hebrew is just this easy. Let's try another word.

גַּד

This word starts with the letter that looks like a guy playing golf "**G**." Add to it the vowel hanging out below it "**ah**." Come back up to the next consonant that looks like a doorway "**D**." Tadaaa! You've read "**GahD**."

"**GahD**" is actually a name. It's the Hebrew name of the **Israelite tribe of Gad**. Now you have a whole new insight into the proper pronunciation of a name you thought you were familiar with. Gad doesn't rhyme with 'had' or 'bad' or 'mad'. It's pronounced "GahD."

ANOTHER FUN LITTLE HEBREW FACT: THERE ARE NO CAPITAL LETTERS IN HEBREW. NO CAPITAL LETTERS TO BEGIN A SENTENCE OR A NAME OR PLACE. THERE ARE NO CAPITAL LETTERS ANYWHERE AT ALL. SO THERE'S A WHOLE SET OF LETTERS YOU WON'T NEED TO LEARN. YAY!

דָג

Next one! Start with the letter that looks like a door "**D**." Add the sound of the vowel below it "**ah**." Come back up to the next consonant that looks like a guy playing golf "**G**." Put it all together and you have "**DahG**."

"**DahG**" means **fish**. Which sounds a lot like the English word dog. But the pronunciation is slightly different. Instead of an "o" sound you're reading an "**ah**" sound. This word is confusing because it sounds almost like dog but don't worry, you'll remember!

WEEK TWO
LESSON ONE

THE LETTER "HEY."

The first letter we're going to learn today is the letter "**Hey.**" It looks like a **House with a Hole** for smoke to escape. It makes the sound of the English letter "**H.**"

THE LETTER "CHET."

It looks almost exactly like the "Hey" with one big difference. It looks like a house WITHOUT a hole for the smoke to escape. And if a house is full of smoke everyone inside will surely begin to choke. And this lovely letter makes a wonderful sound. It sounds like someone choking. Or clearing their throat.

Many other languages (like German for example) have this sound but there is really no sound like this in English. There are some words with this sound from other languages that you may be familiar with. Think about the name of the composer Bach. When you say Bach try this. Lift up the back of your tongue to make the sound of a kitten purring. Now force your breath out while you purr. It's a harsh noise. And you have definitely made everyone around you curious what you're up to.

From what my Spanish speaking students tell me, it's the same sound as the J in Spanish. When I want to write the sound the Chet makes in English, I use the letter combination "CH." But it's not "CH" like chess or chat. It's the "CH" like **BACH**. Keep that in mind when you want to say the name of the letter too. The "CH" in "Chet" is not the "ch" of chess or chat.

Let's read!

חַג

The first letter looks like a house without a hole and we are choking "**CH**." Add on the vowel hanging out below it and we've got an "**ah**" sound. Come back up to the next consonant and we have a guy playing golf "**G**." Put it all together, and we have the Hebrew word "CHahG."

"**CHahG**" means **HOLIDAY** or **FESTIVAL**.

If you want to see it in the original text of the Bible you can! Look at Exodus 12:14.

"And you shall celebrate it as a holiday to God."

The Hebrew text looks like this:

וְחַגֹּתֶם אֹתוֹ חַג לַ-ה'

Handy tip:

When reading from the Hebrew Bible and other holy books you will see extra dots and dashes that are not part of reading in Hebrew. These extra dots and dashes are called cantillation marks. When these holy books are read publicly in the Synagogue the cantillation marks are like musical notes that guide the cantor in singing the words.

For reading purposes these extra dots and dashes are simply ignored. Unless you're studying to be a cantor in a synagogue. But that's for another book.

Look at the third word in the verse above. Remember it's the third word from the right. You can read the word for holiday in Hebrew! In another four and a half weeks, you'll be able to read that entire verse in the original Hebrew. It's inspiring and amazing!

Let's read some more.

הַחַג

The first letter looks like a house with a hole "**H**." The vowel below adds an "**ah**" sound. Back up to the next consonant that looks like a house without a hole and we are choking "**CH**." Then to the vowel hanging below, we have another "**ah**" sound. And finally back up to the top with a cute little guy playing golf "**G**." So we have Hah CHah G. Put it all together and we've got "**HahCHahG**." Which means **THE HOLIDAY** or **THE FESTIVAL**.

IN HEBREW, WHEN YOU WANT TO ADD THE WORD "THE" TO A WORD YOU CAN SIMPLY PREFACE THE WORD WITH A LETTER "HEY." ISN'T THAT CUTE?

הַדָג

Let's walk through it. The first letter looks like a house with a hole "**H**." Followed by a vowel with the sound "**ah**." Next we have the consonant that looks like a door "**D**." With a vowel below it making a sound of "**ah**." The word finishes up with a guy playing golf "**G**." "**Hah-DahG**." Do you remember last class we read the word "DahG"? "DahG" means 'fish'. "**Hah-DahG**" means **THE FISH**. And all we did was add a letter "Hey."

This lesson was a short and sweet one, but it propels us deeper into reading and into the language in general. The classes take a bit of time, but you did it! And you're already seeing results. It's an exciting process!

WEEK TWO
LESSON TWO

THE LETTER "NOON."

At the end of this lesson, you'll be a third of the way through the class. We will have our first bi-weekly review. This class has some awesome Bible quotes too. The first letter for today is the letter "**Noon**." The letter "**Noon**" looks like a **Nose**. It makes the sound of the English letter "**N**." I mentioned earlier that there are no capital letters in Hebrew. But there is a different category of letters that English doesn't have. A small handful of the Hebrew letters have a slightly different look when they are found at the end of a word. These letters are called Final Letters. The letter "Noon" is our first example of a letter with a final version.

The "Final Noon" is ONLY found at the END of a word. It makes the same sound as the regular letter "Noon." It looks like this:

It looks like a Nail being hammered down into the ground. It's kind of like the base of the regular "Noon" was pulled down, and now the whole letter stretches straight down below the line.

Okay now, It's time for a new vowel. So here goes! This vowel is called "**SEGOL.**" It looks like this:

It makes the sound of the English letter combination "**eh.**" Like the "e" sound in the words 'net', 'bed', or 'fed'.

Funny thing is that there is ANOTHER vowel in Hebrew that makes the SAME sound. It's called the "**TZEREH.**" Same sound like the "e" in the words 'net', 'bed' or 'fed'. It looks like this:

So if you see either one, you'll know they both make the "eh" sound.

Let's read!

בֵּן

The first letter looks like a ball in a box "**B**." Hanging below is a vowel that makes an "**eh**" sound. Now let's move back up to the next consonant. It looks like a nail getting hammered into the ground "**N**." Pull it all together and you have the Hebrew word "Behn." "**Behn**" means **son**.

Let's try another word:

חַנָּה

The first letter looks like a house without a hole. Yep, we're choking "**CH**." The vowel below it adds an "**ah**" sound. Let's go back up to the line and we find a letter that looks like a nose "**N**" with a vowel below it that adds the "**ah**" sound. Now the last letter looks like a house with a hole. It adds an "**H**" sound to the end of the word. The H sound is barely audible but it's there. Put it all together and we read "CHahNahH". "**CHah-NahH**" is the original Hebrew version of the name **Hannah**. The prophet Samuel was CHahNahH's son.

Here's a great verse that has TWO words we can already read in the original Hebrew!

I Samuel 1:20

"And it was after a period of days that **CHah-NahH** became pregnant and gave birth to a **son** and called his name Samuel, for he was borrowed from God." The Hebrew text looks like this:

וַיְהִי לִתְקֻפוֹת הַיָּמִים, וַתַּהַר חַנָּה וַתֵּלֶד בֵּן; וַתִּקְרָא אֶת-שְׁמוֹ שְׁמוּאֵל, כִּי מֵ-ה' שְׁאִלְתִּיו.

The fifth and seventh words (from the right!) in the verse above are both words that you can already read! Here's our first example of a cantillation mark. In the letter "Noon" you see an unexpected dot that isn't part of reading the word. Just ignore it.

Let's try some more words.

גַּן

The first letter looks like a guy playing golf with a little "**ah**" vowel hanging out underneath. Followed up by a long letter getting nailed into the ground "**N**." Put it all together and we have "GahN." A "**GahN**" is a **garden**. In modern Hebrew, preschool and kindergarten are called "GahN" as well.

Here's another interesting word.

גַּנָּן

The first letter looks like a guy playing golf with a little "**ah**" vowel hanging out underneath. Followed up by a letter that looks like a nose "**N**" and a vowel "**ah**" hanging out underneath. The final letter at the end of this word looks like a nail getting hammered into the ground "**N**." All these letters together make the word "GahNahN." A "**GahNahN**" is a **gardener**.

הֶגֶה

First we have a house with a hole "**H**" and an "**eh**" vowel hanging out underneath. Then comes a guy playing golf "**G**" with another "**eh**" vowel underneath him. Finally we have a house with a hole at the end of the word "**H**." We read it all together and get "**Heh-GehH**." "**Heh-GehH**" means a **steering wheel**.

Alright. Next, we've got a grand finale to finish up our first two weeks. You're going to amaze yourself. Seriously. Ok. Here goes.

בָּנָנָה

This is exciting. Let's run through it together. The first letter looks like a ball in a box "**B**." Underneath it is an "**ah**" vowel. Back up to the next consonant that looks like a nose "**N**." There's another "**ah**" vowel under that. Back up on the line and we have another consonant that looks like a nose "**N**" with an "**ah**" vowel below it. We've got one last letter at the end of this word that is shaped like a house with a hole "**H**." Now put it all together and you have "BahNahNahH." You guessed it! "**Bah-Nah-NahH**" is Hebrew for **banana**.

AND YOU MY FRIEND,
CAN NOW READ
BANANA IN HEBREW.
SO IN JUST TWO WEEKS
YOU WENT FROM
READING
BANANA IN ENGLISH TO
BEING ABLE TO
READ IT INDEPENDENTLY
IN HEBREW.
INCREDIBLE, RIGHT!?!?!

NOW YOU GET AN ICE
CREAM BREAK! YOU
DESERVE IT.

NNB
AAA ← **BANANA**

START

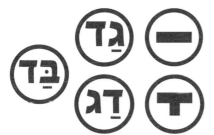

WEEK THREE
LESSON ONE

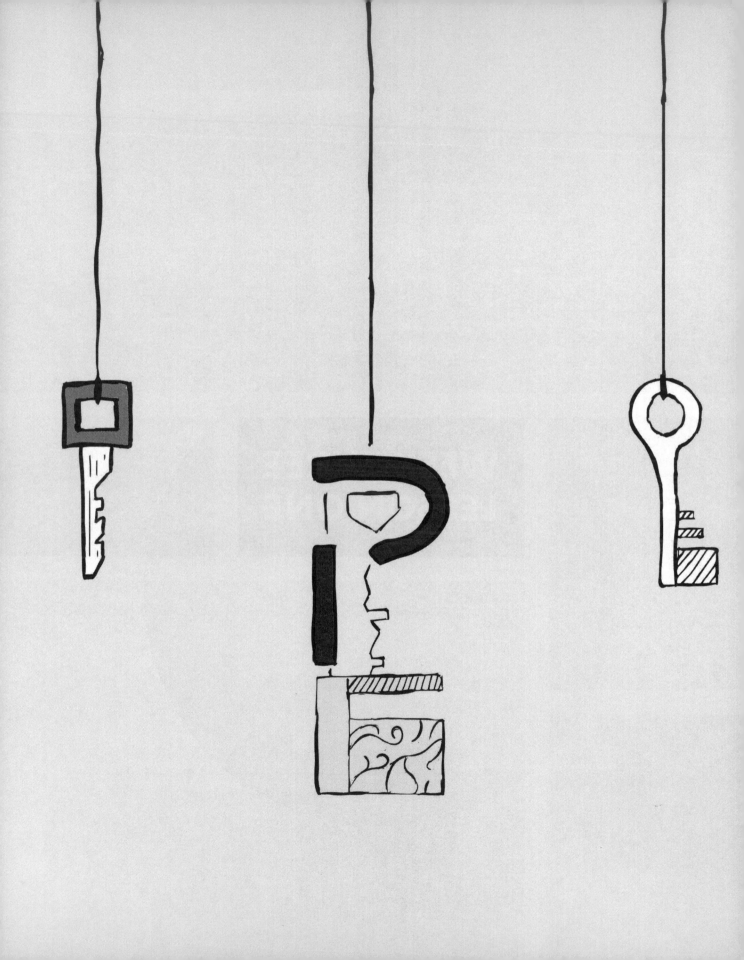

THE LETTER "KOOF."

The letter "**Koof**" looks almost exactly like a **Key**. And that's the sound it makes. The sound of the English letter "**K**."

THE LETTER "SAMECH."

The letter "**Samech**" is **super circular**. It makes the sound of the English letter "**S**."

Let's read some words with these letters and some of the other letters we've already learned.

בָּדַק

Start with the letter that looks like a ball in a box "**B**" followed by the "**ah**" vowel. Next the letter that looks like a door "**D**" with another "**ah**" vowel. Finishing up the word with our new letter that looks like a key "**K**"!

There you have it. The Hebrew word "Bah-DahK." "**Bah-DahK**" means **checked**, like checked on something or someone.

הַדַס

We start with a letter that looks like a house with a hole "**H**" and an "**ah**" vowel. Next the letter that looks like a door "**D**" followed by another "**ah**" vowel. The last letter is our new super circular letter "**S**." Put it all together and you have "Hah-DahS." "**Hah-DahS**" means **myrtle**.

Let's add a "**Hey**" to the end of that word and see what happens.

הַדַסָה

We start with a letter that looks like a house with a hole "**H**" and an "**ah**" vowel. Next the letter that looks like a door "**D**" followed by another "**ah**" vowel. The next letter is our new super circular letter "**S**" followed by another "**ah**" vowel. The word is completed with a letter "**Hey**." Sound it out and you have "Hah-Da-hSahH." "**Hah-Dah-SahH**" is actually one of Queen Esther's names in the Book of Esther.

Esther 2:7

"And he brought up **HahDahSahH**, that is Esther, his uncle's daughter."

וַיְהִי אֹמֵן אֶת-הַדַסָה, הִיא אֶסְתֵּר בַּת-דֹּדוֹ

Look at the fourth word (from the right.) And yes, YOU can read it!

WEEK THREE
LESSON TWO

THE LETTER "MEM." מ

This lesson has some cute letters. We will start with the letter "**Mem**." The letter "**Mem**" looks like a **Mountain with a flag planted** just before the peak. It makes the sound of the English letter "**M**."

The letter "**Mem**" has a final version as well. It looks a lot like the circular "Samech" we learnt about. But it's corners are not rounded. It's corners are, well, corners.

Here it is:

THE LETTER "TET."

We have one more unique letter for today. The letter **"Tet."** The letter **"Tet"** has a lovely **Tail** curling behind it. And it makes the sound of the English letter **"T."**

Now, let's read some words!

קָטָן

The first letter looks like a key "**K**" followed by an "**ah**" vowel. Next comes our new letter with a lovely tail "**T**" paired up with an "**ah**" vowel and finishing with a final letter "**Noon**" looking like a nail being hammered down into the ground. "**Kah-TahN**" means **small or little**.

קֶמַח

The first letter looks like a key "**K**" and is paired with an "**eh**" vowel. Next, you have our new letter shaped like a mountain "**M**" with an "**ah**" vowel hanging below it. Finally, we have a house without a hole "**CH**." "**Keh-MahCH**" means **flour**.

Let's do an easier word.

מַה

Start with our new mountain shaped letter "**M**" with an "**ah**" vowel below and followed by a house with a hole "**H**." Together these letters make the word "**MahH**." "**MahH**" means **what**.

Let's do another easier one.

מָן

Start with our new mountain shaped letter "**M**" with an "**ah**" vowel below and followed by a final letter that looks like a nail being hammered down "**N**." Put it all together and voila "MahN." Do you know what you just read!? "**MahN**" is the original Hebrew word for **manna**. You know, like the food the Israelites ate in the desert. **Manna from heaven**!

Exodus 16:15

"And the children of Israel saw it and they said one to another it's **MahN**."

In Hebrew it looks like this:

וַיִּרְאוּ בְנֵי-יִשְׂרָאֵל, וַיֹּאמְרוּ אִישׁ אֶל-אָחִיו **מָן** הוּא

Can you believe you've been calling it 'Mannah' all this time?

Let's do another word with a Biblical verse.

מַטֶּה

We're starting again with the letter "**Mem**" looking like a mountain "**M**" followed by an "**ah**" vowel. Then a "**Tet**" with a tail "**T**" and an "**eh**" vowel. We finish with a letter "**Hey**" that makes the "**H**" sound. "Mah-TehH." "**Mah-TehH**" means a **stick or a staff**.

Exodus 7:12

"And Aaron's staff swallowed their staffs."

Let's look at it in Hebrew. Pay attention to the second word.

וַיִּבְלַע **מַטֶּה**-אַהֲרֹן, אֶת-מַטֹּתָם.

Isn't this incredible? Here we are at the halfway point of this project. We can read roughly HALF of the letters in the Hebrew language! We are filling in the gaps with every lesson, and the time is flying! With every lesson we are closer to our goal. Keep up the good work!

Bring on the chocolate!

WEEK FOUR
LESSON ONE

O k guys. I've saved this lesson until now, because it's a little tricky. But you've got the basics of Hebrew reading down and I know you're ready for this. This lesson is about silent letters and silent vowels. There are some letters and vowels in Hebrew that don't actually make any sound at all! A different way of thinking about these letters and vowels is to think about them as place holder letters or place holder vowels. The letters and vowels themselves don't make a sound, but you can't always ignore them completely.

Here we go!

THE LETTER "ALEF."

The letter **Alef** is **silent**. It's **all arms and legs, but has no voice.**

THE LETTER "AYIN."

The letter "Ayin" is also silent. You can recognize "Ayin" because he's silently reading a book with his back to you.

Now we're going to do a vowel. "Shva" looks like this:

When you find this vowel hanging below a consonant you try to **halt the flow of the word**. In a similar way to how you halt the flow of words when you come to the end of a sentence or with a **hyphenated word like: up-to-date.**

Here's a tricky thing about "Shva." Sometimes you'll find it hanging out below a consonant TOGETHER with another vowel! Crazy stuff I know. When you see that, just ignore "Shva." That's right, ignore it. Just read the other vowel as if "Shva" isn't even there. Here's what it looks like paired with other vowels:

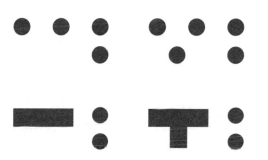

Let's do this!

We've got our silent letter **"Ayin"** reading his book. Hanging out below we have an **"ah"** vowel. So ALL you pronounce is the vowel. Basically ignore the **"Ayin"** and go straight for the vowel **"ah."** Coming back up to the line we have our final letter **"Mem."** Put them together and you have the word **"ahM."** which means **nation**. For example, 'ahM YeeS-Rah-ehL' means nation of Israel.

This time a silent letter **"Alef"** is here, all arms and legs and no voice. So we go straight to the vowel below him **"ah."** Now we come back up to the next consonant that looks like a mountain **"M"** followed by an **"eh"** vowel. The last letter looks like a nail getting hammered down into the ground **"N."** Put it all together and you have such a great word! **"ah-MehN"** means **veritably**. Or in regular English it means **it is true.** "ah-MehN" is the original Hebrew version of the word amen. I bet you've been saying it like "aay-men", haven't you?! Knowing the sounds of the Hebrew vowels make the correct pronunciation more obvious.

Let's do another one with deep significance:

אֶחָד

The silent letter "**Alef**" is skipped right by and the "**eh**" vowel below the "**Alef**" is pronounced. The house without a hole (our chokey letter "**Chet**") is followed by an "**ah**" vowel. And finally the letter "**Daled**" that looks like a door "**D.**" Sound it out "eh-CHahD." In Hebrew "**ehCHahD**" means **one**.

Here's a classic and awesome quote from the Bible in Deuteronomy 6:4

שְׁמַע, יִשְׂרָאֵל: ה' אֱלֹהֵינוּ, ה' אֶחָד

You can read the last word in the verse "ehCHahD."

This verse reads:

"Hear o Israel, The L-rd our G-d the L-rd is **one**."

If you're Jewish, you'll surely recognize this verse as part of the Shema prayer. In Hebrew it sounds like this:

"SH-MahH YeeS-Rah-ehL ah-Do-NahY eh-Loh-Heh-Noo ah-Do-NahY **eh-CHahD**."

These silent letters and vowels have really opened up our reading abilities! There's so many great words to read now that it's hard to stop bringing examples.

עֵדֶן

Our silent letter "**Ayin**" sitting there reading his book is followed by an "**eh**" vowel. Come back up to the line where there's a letter that looks like a door "**D**" with a different "**eh**" vowel below. So far we read "**eh-Deh**." The word finishes up with a final letter "**Noon**" that looks like a nail. "**eh-DehN**" means **Eden like the Garden of Eden**!

Check it out in Genesis 2:15. Pay attention to the eighth word in the verse.

וַיִּקַּח ה' אֱלֹהִים, אֶת-הָאָדָם; וַיַּנִּחֵהוּ בְגַן-עֵדֶן, לְעָבְדָהּ וּלְשָׁמְרָהּ

"G-d took the man and placed him in the garden of **eh-DehN** to work it and guard it."

If you don't already have one, you might want to buy a Hebrew/English Bible with linear translation. I think at this point you'd already enjoy being able to pick out certain words you can read and then just glance across the line to see the translation.

I know we did a lot this lesson, but there's more that I just have to share. This one is from the very last verse in Exodus.

עָנָן

We're starting out again with the silent letter "**Ayin**" this time with an "**ah**" vowel below. Next is a letter that looks like a nose "**N**" with another "**ah**" vowel. Again, our last letter is the final letter "**Noon**", which sounds like?? N! Put it all together. "**ah-NahN**" means "**cloud**".

כִּי עָנָן ה' עַל-הַמִּשְׁכָּן,
יוֹמָם, וְאֵשׁ, תִּהְיֶה לַיְלָה בּוֹ

"For the **cloud** of G-d was on the Tabernacle by day, and fire by night."

With all these great examples from the Bible, we haven't yet had a chance to try out a silent vowel! So let's do that now.

דְּמָמָה

Start with the Daled "**D**" and try to ignore the silent vowel below it, heading straight over to the next consonant. This letter looks like a mountain "**M**" and is followed by an "**ah**" vowel. Coming up to the next consonant, another "**M**" followed by another "**ah**" vowel. And then the last letter is the house with a hole —a barely audible but not silent "**H**". "**D'-MahMahH**" means **silence or stillness**.

Ok, now for the culmination word. The big test. The toughy you'll read like a real live Israelite. How? You'll take it one consonant vowel combination at a time. Enunciate each consonant with it's paired vowel and then move on to the next consonant vowel pair. This word is no more complicated than a much shorter word. Don't try to read it as a whole word. Take it in stages.

נֶאֱמָן

We're starting out with the letter that looks like a nose "**N**" and an "**eh**" vowel below so we read "**Neh**." Then a silent letter with an "**eh**" vowel AND a silent vowel underneath. The ONLY part of this entire combination that you're going to read is the "**eh**" sound. So far we have "**Neh-eh**." Now we go back up to the letter that looks like a mountain "**M**" with an "**ah**" vowel below and finish up the word with a letter we all know at this point - the **"Final Noon**." "**Neh-eh-MahN**" means **faithful**.

WEEK FOUR
LESSON TWO

This lesson basically has a couple of letters with a bunch of different versions of the same letters. It's an easy lesson, but it actually covers a lot. So don't let the easy trick you! You're actually leaping forward.

First up, the letter "Kaf."

THE LETTER "KAF."

The letter "**Kaf**" looks like a poor fellow **Coughing on a Candy**. And it makes the sound of the English letter "**K**."

THE LETTER "CHAF."

The next letter looks exactly like the "Kaf" but with one small difference. It's missing the dot in the middle. This letter is the "**Chaf.**"

It's missing the candy. THIS poor fellow is no longer coughing on the candy. The candy is nowhere to be seen. He's completely **choking** now. And that is the sound the "Chaf" makes. The "**Chaf**" makes the same wonderful **chokey noise** we practiced a few lessons ago with the letter "Chet" (the house without a hole to let the smoke out.)

The letter "Chaf" also has a final version. Meaning, that if there is a "Chaf" at the end of a word the "Chaf" will look a little different. The bottom part of the "Chaf" will be stretched down below the line. You will only ever see this letter at the end of a word. Here is a "**Final Chaf**":

The next letter is a very unique letter. It can be a consonant OR a vowel. One carefully placed dot can transform it. We are about to learn one of the very very very few exceptions to rules of reading. This vowel is found...above the line.

Let's start with it in consonant form.

THE LETTER "VAV."

This is the letter "**Vav**". It makes the sound of the English letter "**V**" and it looks like a **vanilla bean**. It looks exactly like a vanilla bean. So if you've never seen a vanilla bean, google image it right now and you'll never forget the "**Vav**."

Now, sometimes the "Vav" will have a dot directly above it. When it does, the "Vav" becomes the "**Cholam**." It no longer makes the V sound. Now it's a vowel. The "**Cholam**" makes the sound of the English letter combination "**oh**." I like to remember it by a silly facial trick. When I say "**oh**" in a surprised way, my eyebrows always shoot up. And the "**Cholam**" has a dot shooting upwards and makes the sound "**oh**."

Sometimes, you'll see just a dot floating above and between two consonants. It's as if you were seeing the "Cholam", but the "Vav" part is just missing. It makes the same "**oh**" sound. Don't worry, we will see this in some of the word examples below. It's less complicated than it sounds.

At other times the "Vav" will have a dot inside of it. The dot will be sandwiched between the "Vav" and the letter following. At these times the letter "Vav" becomes the vowel "**Shoorook**." "**Shoorook**" makes the sound of the English letter combination "**oo**." I like to picture it as the "Vav" making a kissy face. The sound you make when your lips are puckered up is "**oo**."

One last vowel for today makes the same "**oo**" sound as "Shoorook." This vowel hangs below the line like the bulk of the vowels. It's called "**Koobootz**" and it looks like **three diagonal dots** hanging below a consonant.

Let's get some clarity about all this new info with some reading practice.

Here we have a house without a hole and we are choking "**CH**" followed by an "**ah**" vowel "**CHah**." Back up to the line and we have our new letter that looks like a guy totally choking, no candy in sight "**CH**" followed by another "**ah**" vowel "**Chah-CHah**." Finally, we have a final letter "**Mem**" that brings the word together as "Chah-CHahM." "**Chah-CHahM**" means **wise**.

כֵּן

There's a guy coughing on a candy "**K**" with an "**eh**" vowel below and this short word finishes up with a **"Final Noon."** "**KehN**" is a positive little word that means **yes**!

מְאֹד

First, we have the letter that looks like a mountain with a silent place holder vowel below it. Next we have a silent letter "**Alef**" all arms and legs and no voice. It's voice comes from the **vowel** connected to it. Floating above and between the "Alef" and the letter following is an "**oh**" vowel. Finishing up with a letter that looks like a door "**D**." "**M'-ohD**" means **very**. It's a little word with a few tricky parts. But if you take it consonant vowel by consonant vowel, you can work through it quite successfully!

Let's try an easier one.

הוּא

First you have a house with a hole "**H**" followed by an "**oo**" vowel and finishing up with a silent letter "**Alef**." "**Hoo**" means **he**.

עַמְךָ

Silent letter "**Ayin**" begins the word with an "**ah**" vowel below. Next the letter that looks like a mountain "**M**" with a silent vowel below. "**AhM'**". Then the final letter "**Chaf**" with an "**ah**" vowel. "**ahM'-CHah**" means **your people**.

אָדוֹן

A silent letter "**Alef**" with an "**ah**" vowel and a tricky silent vowel that we're going to completely ignore makes "**Ah.**" Next is a letter that looks like a door "**D**" followed by an "**oh**" vowel. Did you raise your eyebrows? The word finishes with a final letter "**Noon.**" "**ah-DohN**" means **master.**

In modern Hebrew, "ahDohN" means mister. It is used just like like the word mister in English. Mr. Cohen would be ahDohN Cohen. Israelis are very informal though so they only use it that way in extremely formal settings. Also, one of God's names is "ah-Doh-NahY." It is just like "ahDohN" with an extra letter on the end. The last letter changes it's meaning from master to "my Master".

מִיֻחָד

We start out with a letter that looks like a mountain "**M**". A silent vowel is hanging out below. The little yawning "**Yud**" has our new "**Koobootz**" below it and so far we have "**M'-Yoo.**" Next we have a house with no hole "**CH**" and an "**ah**" vowel below followed by the letter that looks like a door "**D**". Put the sounds together and we have "**M'-Yoo-CHahD.**" "**M'-Yoo-CHahD**" means **special.**

NOW YOU CAN READ MOST OF THE LETTERS IN THE HEBREW LANGUAGE. THE LAST TWO LESSONS PUT US WAY AHEAD OF THE GAME. LET'S LOOK AT OUR BI-WEEKLY REVIEW TO SUM UP THE LAST FOUR LESSONS.

הַדַס בָּדַק הֲדַסָּה

מוּ קָטָן מַטֶּה מָה קֶמַח

עֵנָן עֵדֶן אָמֵן דְּמָמָה נֶאֱמָן עַם אֶחָד

חָכָם

אָדוֹן הוּא מְאֹד

עִמְּךָ מְיֻחָד כֵּן

WEEK FIVE
LESSON ONE

THE LETTER "RESH."

The letter "**Resh**" is my personal favorite. It's my favorite mostly because it's got a sweet picture. The "**Resh**" looks like a **Rainbow** and makes the sound of the English letter "**R**."

THE LETTER "FEY."

Now the letter "**Fey**" has a really unique shape. It looks just like a **Face** and makes the sound of the English letter "**F**."

THE LETTER "PEY."

There are a handful of letters in the Hebrew alphabet that have sister letters with an added dot somewhere. The letter "Fey" has a sister letter with an added dot. It's called the letter "**Pey.**" The letter "**Pey**" makes the sound of the English letter "**P**" and looks like a **face with a Pimple**.

The letter "**Fey**" also has a final version. This is found only at the end of a word. The "**Final Fey**" looks just like the "**Fey**" but the bottom of the letter is pulled down below the line.

רָאָה

The first letter looks like a rainbow "**R**" with an "**ah**" vowel below. Next is a silent letter "**Alef**" with an "**ah**" vowel below. Finally we have a barely audible "**Hey.**" Put it together and we have "**Rah-ahH**" which means **saw**. Like, "he saw her at the store".

סוּף

We're starting out with a circular letter "**Samech**" followed with an "**oo**" vowel and finishing up with a "Final Fey." "**SooF**" means **reeds**.

Here's a fun fact. Ever heard of the Red Sea? Well, it's actually not red at all. In the Bible it's called the "**YahM SooF**" or the **Sea of Reeds**. And guess what? It does have reeds in it. Since the days before autocorrect a basic mistake was made and has lived on for generations. For the simple reason that people rely on translations of books. Even books as important to them as the Bible! There are plenty more (and more meaningful) basic mistakes like that one. Good for you for taking the initiative to learn on your own!

סֵפֶר

Starting again with our circular letter "**Samech**" followed with an "**eh**" vowel. Next we have our letter that looks like a face "**F**" with an "**eh**" vowel below. A rainbow shaped letter "**R**" finishes up this word. Put it together and you have "Seh-FehR." "**Seh-FehR**" means **book**.

Let's do a word with a Bible quote.

פַּרְעֹה

First we have a letter that looks like a face with a pimple "**P**" with an "**ah**" vowel hanging out below. Next, our rainbow shaped letter "**R**" with a silent place holder vowel below it. So far we have "**PahR'**." Next we have a silent letter "**Ayin**" with an "**oh**" vowel floating between it, and the final letter shaped like a house with a hole "**H**." "**PahR'-ohH**" is the Hebrew word for **Pharaoh**. As in the **king of Egypt**.

Exodus 2:5

וַתֵּרֶד בַּת-פַּרְעֹה לִרְחֹץ עַל-הַיְאֹר

"And **PahR-ohH's** daughter went down to bathe in the river."

Let's finish this lesson with an easy word.

פֶּה

The first letter looks like a face with a pimple "**P**" with an "**eh**" vowel hanging below and a letter "**Hey**" finishing up the word "**H**." "**PehH**" means **mouth**.

WEEK FIVE
LESSON TWO

With the letters we're learning In this lesson we're going to be able to read (at least) one truly epic word. Really.

THE LETTER "LAMED."

The letter "**Lamed**" has a **Lap** and makes the sound of the English letter "**L**."

THE LETTER "TAF."

The letter "Taf" makes the sound of the English letter "T." There is another letter we learned that also makes the "T" sound. No worries. It's the same exact sound. Nothing new here, except a new look for the same sound.

The "Taf" looks a lot like the "Chet" and the "Hey." But there's one difference that sets it apart AND helps you remember it's sound. It has a big TOE sticking out!

THE LETTERS "SHIN AND SIN." שִׂ שִׁ

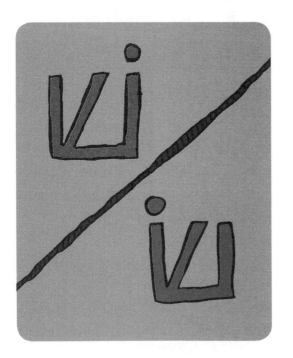

The next two letters look almost the same. They are called "**Shin**" and "**Sin**." The "**Shin**" makes the sound of the English letter combination "**Sh**." The "**Sin**" makes the sound of the English letter "**S**." How can you tell these twins apart? The "**Shin**" has a **dot on the top right** and the "**Sin**" has a **dot on the top left**.

Remember this nifty little saying and you won't get mixed up:

IF IT'S NOT RIGHT, IT'S A SIN.

Let's start with an easy word.

לֹא

Start the word with the "**Lamed**" with the lap followed by the floating "**oh**" vowel and then a silent "**Alef**." "**Loh**" means **no**.

שַׁבָּת

The dot on the letter is on the right so we know it's not a "Sin", so it must be a "**Shin**". With an "**ah**" vowel hanging out below we have "**SHah**". Next our ball in a box "**B**" with another "**ah**" vowel. Now we have "**SHah-Bah**." Let's finish it up with our new letter "**Taf**" with it's big toe sticking out and we have "**SHah-BahT**"! "**SHah-BahT**" means **Saturday**. It also means "**Sabbath**"!

In Hebrew the first six days of the weeks don't actually have names. Sunday is called "YohM Ree-SHohN", which means, "first day". Monday is called "YohM SHeh-Nee", or "second day". The only day with a name of it's own is Saturday which is called "SHah-BahT" which literally means "He rested."

שָׂרָה

On this first letter the dot is not on the right, so we know it's a "**Sin**." An "**ah**" vowel hangs below it and is followed by a rainbow shaped letter "**R**" with an "**ah**" vowel below it. Finishing up with a "**Hey**" house with a hole "**H**." And we have "Sah-RahH." A slightly different pronunciation of Sarah. "**Sah-RahH**" was **Abraham's wife**.

And now for a very important word!

תּוֹרָה

First thing to notice is the toe sticking out "**T**" followed by an "**oh**" vowel. Next, we have a rainbow shaped letter "**R**" with an "**ah**" vowel hanging below. At the end of the word a letter "**Hey**." The "**Toh-RahH**" is the **first five books of the Bible**! You can read the word "Toh-RahH" in the original Hebrew text! THAT is awesome!

We are almost done. I can't even believe how little there is left to learn. Sure, you'll need to keep practicing. But you've got almost all the tools now.

BREAK FOR MILKSHAKE! YOU'VE WORKED HARD!

WEEK SIX
LESSON ONE

THE LETTER "YUD."

Finally, we get to cute little "Yud." When my kids were learning to read, their teacher called it "baby Yud". "Yud" looks like a little Yawn and makes the sound of the English letter "Y."

Here's another vowel. It is just one little dot that hangs below the line. It's called "**Cheereek**" and makes the sound of the English letter combination "**ee**."

THE LETTER "TZADDIK."

The next letter is called a "**Tzaddik.**" It makes a sound found very rarely in the English language. The sound is the same sound as the **two z's** in the word pizza. Or the combination of the **t and the s** in **Pat's Place**. It helps to say the words out loud to get a better idea of the sound I'm talking about.

There is also a "**Final Tzaddik**" that looks just like "Tzaddik" except the bottom part of the letter is stretched down below the line. And of course the "**Final Tzaddik**" makes the same sound as the "**Tzaddik**" and is **ONLY found at the end of a word**.

ץ

Let's try out our new letters.

יָד

Cute little yawning "**Yud**" followed by an "**ah**" vowel and finishing with a letter that looks like a door "**D**." And this spells "YahD." "**YahD**" means **hand**.

צָרִיךְ

First we have our "**Tzaddik**" followed by an "**ah**" vowel "**TZah**." Next comes a letter like a rainbow followed by our new "**ee**" vowel "**Tzah-Ree**." We finish up with our "**Final Chaf**". "**TZah-Ree-CH**" means **need**.

בַּיִת

The letter that looks like the ball in the box "**B**" followed by an "**ah**" vowel. Now we have a seemingly tricky combo that is the yawning "**Yud**" followed by an "**ee**" vowel. Together they make "**Yee**." Finish it up with a letter with a big toe "**T**." "**Bah-YeeT**" means **house** or **home**.

מַצָה

The letter that looks like a mountain "**M**" with an "**ah**" vowel hanging below. Followed by a "**Tzaddik**" and an "**ah**" vowel and finishing up with a house with a hole "**H**." "**Mah-TZahH**" is **unleavened bread** that Jews eat on Passover.

אֶרֶץ

A silent letter "**Alef**" with an "**eh**" vowel followed by a rainbow shaped letter "**R**" and another "**eh**" vowel and finishing off with a "**Final Tzaddik**." "**eh-RehTZ**" means **land** or **country**.

Are you ready for a wonderful word?

יִשְׂרָאֵל

Yawning "**Yud**" with an "**ee**" vowel hanging below followed by a "**Sin**" (the dot is not on the right) with a **silent place holder vowel**, So far we have "**Yees**". Then comes a rainbow shaped letter with an "**ah**" vowel. Next, we have a silent letter "**Alef**" with an "**eh**" vowel and the word finishes with a letter with a lap "**L**." All together we have "YeeS-Rah-ehL." "**YeeS-Rah-ehL**" means **Israel**!

NOW THAT YOU KNOW IT'S NOT PRONOUNCED "IZ-REE-EL" BUT "YEES-RAH-EL" YOU MAY JUST WANT TO FORGET THE FINAL LESSON! BOOK A FLIGHT AND PACK YOUR BAGS FOR THE HOLY LAND.

WEEK SIX
LESSON TWO

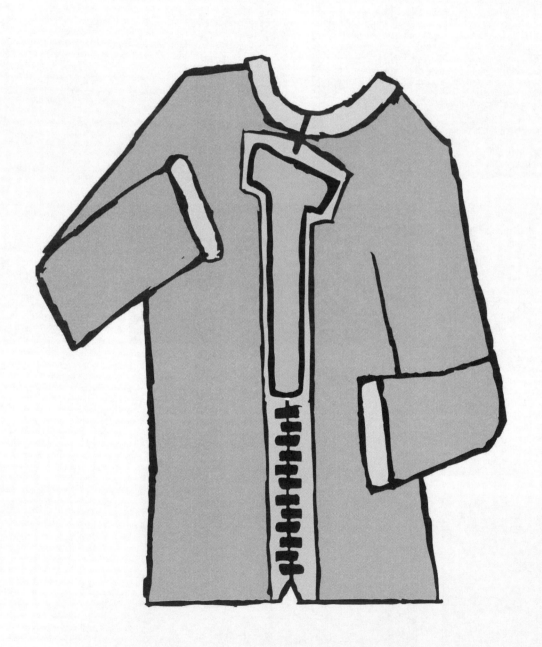

THE LETTER "ZAYIN."

"Zayin" is a letter that's been left for last for no good reason at all! It makes the sound of the English letter "Z" and looks like a Zipper.

THE LETTER "VET."

The first letter we learned way back when was the letter "Bet", the ball in a box. Well "Bet" has a sister letter with no ball. It's called "**Vet**." The "**Vet**" just has a **Vacant Void** where the ball should be. It makes the sound of the English letter "**V**."

Here's a real exception to our reading rules. The one exception: When you see a **"Chet"** (house without a hole) with a **"patach"** (the **"ah"** vowel that is just one horizontal line) at the **END** of a word, instead of pronouncing it "CHah" you pronounce it **"ahCH."**

Let's see it in action.

יָרֵחַ

Little yawning **"Yud"** with an **"ah"** vowel followed by a rainbow shaped letter **"R"** with an **"eh"** vowel makes **"Yah-Reh."** The final two sounds are the **"Chet"** **"Patach"** combo we talked about **"ahCH."** All together we read **"Yah-Reh-ahCH"** which means **moon.**

רוּחַ

Start out with a rainbow shaped letter **"R"** followed by an **"oo"** vowel. The **"Chet"** **"Patach"** combo finishes this short word with **"ahCH."** Together it spells **"Roo-ahCH"** which means **wind** or **spirit.**

זֶה

Zipper shaped **"Zayin"** has an **"eh"** vowel below and is followed by a **"Hey."** **"ZehH"** means **this.**

Let's do a longer word now. It's long, but not difficult because we're going to take it one step at a time!

עֲבוֹדָה

Silent letter **"Ayin"** reading his book with an **"ah"** vowel and a **silent vowel** hanging below. Followed by a letter with a vacant void **"Vet"** and an **"oh"** vowel right after it. So far we have **"ahVoh.** Next a letter that looks like a door **"D"** with an **"ah"** vowel below and finally a letter **"Hey"** at the end **"H."** Combine it all and we have **"ah-Voh-DahH"** which means **work.**

YOU'VE WORKED HARD TO GET TO THIS POINT AND I'M SO PROUD!

זֶבְרָה

Starting out with the letter that looks like a zipper "**Z**" with an "**eh**" vowel. Next a ball in a box with a **silent place holder vowel** below. Now, a rainbow shaped letter "**R**" with an "**ah**" vowel followed by a "**Hey.**" All together it makes "ZehB-Rah." And guess what? "**ZehB-Rah**" means **zebra**.

Now for the word you've been waiting for for six weeks! The best of the best. The highlight of highlights. Get your celebration plans ready!

עִבְרִית

Starting out with a silent letter "**Ayin**" reading his book with an "**ee**" vowel hanging out below. A vacant void "**Vet**" had a silent vowel below "**eeV'**." Followed by a rainbow shaped letter "**R**" with an "**ee**" vowel underneath and finally a letter with a toe sticking out "**T**." "**eeV'-ReeT**" means **HEBREW**!!!!!!!!!!!!!!!!!!!!

רָאָה סֵפֶר פ
סוֹף פֶּה פַּרְעֹה

שַׁבָּת תּוֹרָה
שָׂרָה לֹא

יִשְׂרָאֵל מַצָּה אֶרֶץ צ
צָרִיך בַּיִת יָד •

יָרֵחַ רוּחַ חַ
זֶה
עֲבוֹדָה עִבְרִית זֶבְרָה

ו (V)	ה (H)	ד (D)	ג (G)	ב (V)	בּ (B)	א (silent)
ז (CH)	ח (CH)	כ (K)	י (Y)	ט (T)	ח (CH)	ז (Z)
ע (silent)	ס (S)	ן (N)	נ (N)	ם (M)	מ (M)	ל (L)
ר (R)	ק (K)	ץ (TZ)	צ (TZ)	ף (F)	פ (F)	פּ (P)
ת (T)	תּ (T)	שׂ (S)	שׁ (SH)			

| וֹ (oh) | ׃ (stop) | ֵ (eh) | ֳ (eh) | ָ (ah) | ָ (ah) |
| ֶ (eh) | ַ (ah) | ֲ (ah) | ֻ (oo) | וּ (oo) | ִ (ee) |

LET'S CELEBRATE!

You! You now have the tools to read ANY word in Hebrew. You know every vowel, every consonant, and you know the few tricks there are. You've got mnemonic tools to help you remember the letters and they'll keep the language alive in your mind. You've conquered the most challenging part of the Hebrew language. With practice, your comfort in reading will grow, and before long you'll be able to read in Hebrew as smoothly as you read in English.

In fact, when you gain some practice, you'll get a feel for the rhythm of the language and it'll become so familiar that you'll even be able to read without vowels. In Israel today, most of the newspapers and books are printed without vowels! The mind is an amazing thing. Learning new skills is so valuable. I'm really happy you chose to spend your time, effort, and energy learning to read Hebrew with me. Thank you! And congratulations on your new and awesome life skill! **YOU can read Hebrew**!

TAKE IT AWAY!

בְּרֵאשִׁית בָּרָא אֱלֹהִים אֵת הַשָּׁמַיִם וְאֵת הָאָרֶץ

B-R'ehSHeet BahRah 'ehLohHeeYM 'ehT HaSHahMahYeeM V-'ehT Hah'ahRehTZ

In the beginning God created the heavens and the earth.

A VERY SERIOUS AND IMPORTANT NOTE

I've tried to keep this book really fun and cute, but now it's time for something totally serious.

Now that you know how to read every letter and vowel combination, you need to know something very important. There is one word in the Hebrew language that is written but never, ever said aloud. The special name of God. When we come across this holy name we are careful never to say it aloud.

Actually we never pronounce any of God's Hebrew names in regular conversation. Instead we say "**Hah-SHehM**" which just means **The Name**. But we do pronounce them in prayer or when reading from the Torah.

But this special name of God is so awesome and holy that it is **never, ever pronounced, even in prayer**. Instead, whenever we see it in the Torah or in a prayer book we substitute it with the name "**ah-Doh-NaiY**." "**ah-Doh-NaiY**" means "**my Master**."

In the Bible you will see this special name of God written like this:

In the prayer book you will often see it written in an abbreviated form like this:

The written name of God is a holy word. Something with the name of God written on it should be treated with respect. It shouldn't be left on the floor or thrown in the trash. That's why I've had the name printed here pixelated and also written it in a hyphenated form.

So we end this book in the spirit of what
King Solomon said:

**"THE END OF THE MATTER, ALL
HAVING BEEN HEARD: FEAR GOD,
AND KEEP HIS COMMANDMENTS;
FOR THIS IS THE WHOLE MAN"
—KOHELET 12:13**

This book was made possible by the following generous supporters

Mark and Diane Cowhy
Shirli Reed/Batya Sasson
Patricia Barragan
Wendy L. Boyd
Janet and Bernie Buckman
Darnell Clayton
Bill Cohen
Sylvia D. Davis
Brian and Cary Densow
Lisa Dotson
Sarah Laks Einhorn
Finbarr Farragher
Dee Dee Felton
Tammy Folsom
Jeremy Gaston
Sandra Geliga
Debbie Ingle
Sharon and Andrew McCann
Multz Family
Ann and Ted Palesky
Erick Parodi Macias
Gary A. Peabody
Ronda Leigh Rooker
Lisa Gale Slaughter
Teresa Summers Cerna
Renee Tibbetts
Tommie L. Turner
Diane Varsek
Marjorie Zimmerman

ABOUT THE AUTHOR

Miiko Shaffier was born in Florida in 1978. She grew up mostly in Canada and spent some time living in both New York and California. She married Aaron in 2000, and in 2007 they immigrated to Israel with their young family.

Miiko now lives in Be'er Sheva the city of Abraham with her husband and nine children. Aside from teaching Hebrew reading, Miiko is a certified Pilates instructor.